SCILLY PECULIAR

a collection comic and curious

CLIVE MUMFORD

DYLLANSOW TRURAN

Published by Dyllansow Truran 2000

Croft Prince, Mount Hawke, Truro TR4 8EE

Copyright Clive Mumford © 2000

Cover illustration Terry McKenna

Line drawings Sue Lewington
Copyright Dyllansow Truran © 2000

Printed and bound in Cornwall
R Booth (Bookbinders) Ltd & Troutbeck Press
Antron Hill, Mabe, Penryn TR10 9HH

ISBN 1 85022 133 2

Never on Sunday

There is no flying or steamer to Scilly on Sundays so the local newsagent is unable to get his papers. The following is a typical exchange in the Hugh Town paper shop on a Sunday morning:

Visitor: Good morning. The "Sunday Times", please.

Newsagent: I'm sorry, sir, we have no Sunday newspapers.

Visitor: What are these? (pointing to papers on the counter).

Newsagent: Yesterday's.

Visitor: When do you get today's?

Newsagent: Tomorrow.

Visitor: What about tomorrow's?

Newsagent: With today's.

Visitor: When?

Newsagent: Tomorrow. You wouldn't expect to get tomorrow's papers today would you?

Responsibility

The sheer enormity of what he had just done hit the islander like a sledgehammer. Worse for drink he had driven to his home "in the country" on St.Mary's, bouncing off one hedge, only narrowly avoiding the other. So he got back into the car, drove back to the pub, parked the car and walked home ...as any responsible man would do.

Hawser's length

A celebrated island eccentric of yesteryear had the perfect answer to the vexed business of paying rates. He ignored 'em. He lived permanently in a boat, the *Mahana*, moored at a hawser's length from the Old Quay, St.Mary's. He reasoned that as he was not a resident on the parish land he, therefore, had no obligation to the Town Hall exchequer. A singular character was Harold Sandrey, Italian consular agent, Lloyd's agent and auctioneer.

First motor boat

The first motor boat in Scilly - the *Cambridge* - was owned by Bertie Mumford, proprietor of the now gone Holgate's Hotel, St.Mary's. He fitted an engine to a boat from the Falklands which was wrecked on the Bishop in 1901. To the Air Force in the Great War is credited the introduction of the motor car.

A Scillonian first 'down under'

A Scillonian is thought to have discovered Australia, native aboriginals apart, of course. He was said to have been a St.Agnes seaman, a Hicks, naturally: one Zachaiah Hicks who was the look-out aboard Captain Cook's *Endeavour*, when the coastline of Australia first hove into view. That first landfall is perhaps better known as Cape Everard. It is also known as Point Hicks.

Not worth its salt

Before the coming of the island's desalination plant St.Mary's would annually lurch into water crisis at the high summer peak of tourist demand. As an experiment a cargo of fresh water was brought over in *RMV Scillonian's* ballast tanks. The pumping of the water from the quay to the Buzza Hill reservoir provided an exercise for the local fire brigade - and interest to islander and visitor alike. The water engineer tried some before pumping it into the catchment and spat it out. It was tainted with salt and had to be ditched.

The hatbox

Legend has it that the world famous Isles of Scilly flower industry owes its origins to a humble hatbox. Rocky Hill farmer William Trevellick is said to have packed some narcissi into this millinery accessory and, purely speculatively, sent it to Covent Garden, London. The return exceeded expectation. The flower industry was up and running.

Savages

It seems Scillonians were once perceived as savages! When the *SS Deleware* was wrecked in 1871, Bryher islanders mounted an epic rescue. They carried a gig overland from one side of Bryher to the other, launched her, rowed her to Samson, carried her across the waist of that island, relaunched her and pulled to the stranded survivors. The latter had gathered a pile of stones to fend off what they believed to be barbarians.

What's in a name?

During the dark days of the Second World War the town and country units of the St.Mary's Home Guard were called to the eastern side of the island because of reports of an invasion. Intent on repelling Nazi boarders, they rushed to the map reference - Normandy - a country area on St.Mary's. In France D-Day was starting.

A policeman's lot

In the late 19th century law enforcement on St.Mary's was done - or not done - by islanders "made up" to the dubious position of constable. They were given a meagre stipend, a helmet, truncheon and told to get on with it. This ad hoc arrangement was decidedly "iffy" in law and almost certainly challengeable in the courts. The turnover of constables was heavy. A number were summarily dismissed because of "profane language", "lewd conduct" or "drunkenness".

The ever open gate

The most redundant protective device in the whole world is at St.Mary's airport in the Isles of Scilly. It is a gate - a forever open gate - a barrier which has never been closed. It was installed in the wake of the new hard-surface tarmac runway as a security measure and also to prevent the precious strip from being used as an extra-curricular racetrack for burn-ups. Keyholders are legion, entry commonplace.

Underwater lumber yard

The St.Mary's woodworker can draw on a lumber yard with a difference - a submarine one. An islander has acquired the rights of the cargo of the *Fantee* wrecked on the Sevenstones in 1949. She carried West African hard wood - great baulks of timber ranging from mahogany, opepe, iroko, aphselia. They lie on the seabed, perfectly preserved under a marine crust. When the woodworker wants material a diver brings some logs to the surface and they are towed into Porthmellon.

Mistaken guns

It was the well established practice for east-bound transatlantic liners in the 19th century to fire their guns when passing Scilly in order to alert their agent ashore of their pending arrival in a mainland port. The agent would telegraph ahead. In 1875 distress guns were mistakenly taken for this signalling practice and there was no initial response to the German ship *Schiller*'s trouble on the Retarrier Ledges. She went down and with her over 300 souls.

Tall story?

It is said a Scillonian seaman aboard the ill-fated *HMS Association* in 1707 had the temerity to advise Admiral Sir Clowdisley Shovell that his fleet was dangerously off course. For a man before the mast to suggest to his betters, that they did not know their latitude from their longitude, was mutiny. He was duly hanged from the yardarm after most generously being allowed to recite the 23rd Psalm. Within moments of his demise the *Association* struck the Gilstone and everyone on board perished. So who was around to tell the tale of the Scillonian seaman?

Smoking the pipe of peace

The longest "war" in history had as one of its unlikely participants the Isles of Scilly. It is said that during the confusions of the 17th century English Civil War, Admiral Van Tromp, of broom-to-the-masthead fame, declared war on the islands - and sailed off into history. Holland and tiny Scilly have therefore been on a war footing ever since, even if they didn't know it! In the 1980s the then chairman of the Islands' Council Roy Duncan decided this lamentable state of affairs should end. He conceived - and brokered - the brilliant publicity wheeze of inviting the Dutch plenipotentiary, no less, over to Scilly to smoke the peace pipe. Terms were agreed, hostilities formally brought to an end, the three centuries-old hatchet buried. The path was smoothed for receipt of the Dutch tourist.

Off target!

The most spectacularly bad piece of map reading in military history - or its best example of effective sabotage - has to be the affair of the Parliamentarian attack on Tresco during the 17th Century Civil War. In a night-time attack they, in error, invaded the tiny uninhabited island of Northwethel, finding nothing more hostile there than a few seagulls and rabbits. It is said that a local pilot called Nance - a royalist sympathiser - ensured the confusion!

Depressing

One of the more impotent military structures to have been erected in Scilly down the years must surely be King Charles' Castle on Tresco. It was sited to command the adjacent Tresco Channel but its guns would not sufficiently depress to be effective! Cromwell's Castle, which came later and was better sited, did the trick.

The twitcher phenomenom

For centuries rare birds had been visiting Scilly unnoticed and, therefore, unrecorded until the modern "twitcher" phenomenon put the islands on the birders' itinerary. Now, annually, Scilly is an autumn Mecca for birders who come in their thousands. It is said the colourfully-named Yellow Bellied Sapsucker started it all. It would, wouldn't it, with a name like that! Strange tales of twitching are legion: for example the recent mega twitch to see the Spotless Starling - a first for Britain. It turned out to be just a common starling although its markings were so contradictory there was talk of trapping it and taking a DNA! Then there was the time when hundreds of twitchers, telescopes in serried ranks, were observing a rarity on the Garrison - not for long - a tabby emerged from the undergrowth and despatched it before their horrified eyes.

Unique

Scilly's Unitary Authority, now over 100 years old, is unique. A community of parish pump size - that of a mainland village - is administered by a council with District, County and City powers. It owns and runs its own airport, is the country's sole public sector water undertaking, a Coastal Defence Authority, and an LEA, apart from discharging statutory obligations in social services, planning, housing and many others.

Redundant

The Islands' council housing committee is a model of redundancy. It cannot - indeed is not allowed to - execute its primary function of housing allocation, even if there are any houses to allocate and there are very few. Legislation decrees a councillor cannot adjudicate on a housing applicant who lives in the same ward. St.Mary's is all one ward therefore, en bloc, the committee cannot function in this sphere. Allocations are now done by the office staff - based, of course, on councillors' policy.

Listed loos

The business of categorising the worth of Scillonian buildings is seen by many as, at best arbitrary, at worst downright crazy. Take the case of the Strand lavatories. Or perhaps you had better not. For years there has been talk, just talk, mind you, of replacing them. Shabby, rundown they have been labelled: an affront to hygiene. It is said half of nearby Town Beach silts up the urinals and that its cisterns are served by mooring chains nicked from the beach. The building is listed!

Crowning glory

As a unitary authority Scilly's council wields extensive powers, but visitors most be puzzled by the claim that their powers extend to crowning monarchs. The plaque on the shelter in the Strand on St.Mary's says it was erected " to commemorate the Coronation of Queen Elizabeth II BY THE COUNCIL OF THE ISLES OF SCILLY ".

Wooden horse

Isles of Scilly Council planners were recently asked to approve an application to build a - wooden horse shelter - and they gave it.

Bill payer

An islander was reputed to have the perfect solution to the problem of paying bills. Once a month he would place all the demands in his pork pie hat and select one for payment. If it was too much, he returned the bill to the hat and waited another month. Egbert Nicholas Mumford found the system ideal. His creditors didn't.

Aviation mystery

An enduring mystery relating to aviation during the Second World War has been solved. A civilian Dragon plane, carrying passengers from St.Mary's to Land's End, disappeared without trace. It was assumed she had crashed. Aviation historian Mike Ingham - well known in the islands - discovered that it was shot down by German fighters returning to France from an abortive sortie in the Irish Sea. They mistook the Dragon's markings for a "hostile". Mr Ingham's definitive account of the tragedy was published in "Air Enthusiast".

Marooned

Just after the Second World War a well known BBC broadcaster was sent on an assignment to Scilly's Bishop Rock Lighthouse as part of a nation-wide 1946 Christmas Day link-up of Britain's peripheral regions. Edward Ward should have been on the "Rock" a matter of mere hours. Bad weather set in. The boat, which did the Trinity House relief, was unable to take him off. He was eventually "rescued" by the St.Mary's lifeboat after being marooned for over three weeks!

Keep it under your hat!

The transatlantic liner *Minnehaha*, which was wrecked on Scilly Rock in 1910, carried a wide range of cargo, notably cash registers, auto parts, sewing machines, typewriters and tobacco. She also carried the very latest in *haute couture* millinery. Soon island women, hitherto not known for high fashion, were sporting the most outrageous hats. Their response in Hugh Street to a compliment about their new headwear? A triumphant "Ha-Ha"!

Jewellery hoist

History's most incompetent jewellery hoist took place in Scilly not many years ago when a mainlander - fuelled by the Christmas spirit - haphazardly chucked a brick through a Hugh Town shop window and scarpered (unsteadily) with the booty. The next day it was duly found under his mattress and strewn around his bedroom. The hoist was doomed from the outset. Being Christmas there was no way in or out of the islands by air or sea!

Two in a bed

A well-loved island doctor of yesteryear liked a drop or two. One night, worse for wear, he was called to the bedside of a portly farmer suffering from a stomach ailment. "I feel awful, doc" the patient moaned to the figure teetering over him. "That makes two of us" came the reply. "Move over". And the doctor got into bed with him!

Truancy

The Islands' Secretary for Education had, as a statutory - and superfluous -

duty, to check tiny 8-pupil St.Agnes school for truancy. He found irregularity, all right - surfeit instead of deficit. Tiny tots had joined their elder brothers and sisters – willingly!

Narrow escape

A regular visitor to Scilly joined salvagers at the wreck of the *S.S. Plympton* on the Lethegus Rocks to the back of St.Agnes in 1909. The steamer was carrying Indian corn from Rosario in Brazil to Dublin. The visitor was down in the captain's cabin when she slipped off the rock and went down. The water pressure was such that it shot him to the surface. In his hand he held the captain's dinner bell! The shock of his narrow escape subsequently turned his hair white!

Hot bed of crime

Such is the high crime rate in Scilly that in 1997/8 the magistrates court, which meets on the first Friday of every month, did not convene for seven months due to lack of "business". During this time the Islands' council statutorily - and ironically - had to address the Government's 'Crime and Disorder Bill'!

Fore! plane sighted

Before the present airport at High Cross, St.Mary's, was established Scillonian aviation had to make do with the fairways of the island's golf links. Golfers were warned of the imminent arrival of "flying machines " - as they were memorably described at the time by a leading islander ("atrocities" was another!) - by the ringing of a bell. They would then discard their niblicks or mashies and assume the role of ad hoc airport staff by holding down the wings in high winds! During the war the links were also used to train hawks to intercept carrier pigeons with messages from Nazi spies.

The coast was clear

The scenario at the wreck of the container ship *Cita* at Porth Hellick, St.Mary's in 1997 was one that salvagers the world over dream of. The police sergeant was absent on the mainland. There was no Customs and Excise Officer. There was no Chief coastguard. The coast was clear, very clear, indeed and Scillonians knew it.

Out in the cold!

When the Isles of Scilly Council voted to make their properties "no smoking" they extended the ban to St.Mary's Airport. However they generously made a concession to the travelling puffer - not by allocating a smoking zone but by providing an ashtray - fixed to an outside wall!

Smart move!

Bus drivers were miffed more than somewhat when a motion was carried by a council committee to call for smarter dress. This was Scilly, not Savile Row, they reasoned. Passengers never complained when they had to get out and push the bus when it broke down and the newsagent didn't mind having to circumvent an oar propping open a defective boot in order to get to his papers. They duly turned up for work in – dinner jackets!

Demolition job

An off-island lady came down to St.Mary's to brush up her driving technique before a planned mainland motoring holiday. She hired a car, turned on the engine, engaged gear - and immediately demolished the only traffic hazard on the whole island. What remained of the bollard was mounted by some wags above St.Mary's quay steps when she returned to her off-island home.

Gone fishin'

During the Second World War a small Hurricane flight was stationed at St.Mary's airport. Its code name was appropriate: "Gone Fishin". It combated German hostile planes like Dorniers, Heinkels and Messerschmitt. One pilot was tragically lost when, as a prank, he attempted to fly between the masts of the steamer *Scillonian* and plunged into the sea. In the First World War there was a seaplane base on Tresco.

Priceless ring

Before the corpse of Admiral Sir Clowdisley Shovell was buried in a rough grave above Porth Hellick beach, St.Mary's after the 1707 shipwreck disaster of *HMS Association*, legend has it that an island woman beachcomber relieved a finger of a priceless emerald ring. The admiral, exhumed, later turned up at Westminster Abbey, a more appropriate resting-place. The ring never did - officially, that is.

Desert isle conference

Perhaps the most unusual Press Conference in British political history was held in Scilly in the early 1960s. Lord Wilson, then plain Harold Wilson - newly elected, pipe-smoking Labour Prime Minister - met the media on the beach of deserted island of Samson dressed in shorts and sandals.

No M.O.T

There is no MOT or speed limit in Scilly. There are nine miles of roads on St.Mary's and anything up to 800 vehicles. Before Euro environmental strictures stopped the time-honoured practice old wrecks would be pushed over the cliff at Deep Point to form convenient habitats for lobsters. Nowadays they are shipped out as scrap to the mainland.

Weighed and found wanting!

Post-war, in 1946, a St.Mary's farmer acquired a licence from the British Boxing Board of Control to stage a show in the Town Hall. The fighters duly assembled at noon for the traditional and obligatory weigh-in. There were no scales. The old fashioned penny-in-the-slot variety, located outside the chemists, saved the day. It was carried to the Town Hall - by the boxers.

Penalised for being squeaky clean!

The successful detection of fraud - a statutory requirement for any council - has an absurd bearing on the Isles of Scilly Authority's funding allocation. If they do not find any, they are deemed not to be doing their job and are fiscally penalised! They have great difficulty in discovering fraud in the islands. Scilly is so small and knowledge so intimate that would-be fraudsters can be effectively deterred at source. Yet for this prevention rather than cure approach the islands' exchequer suffers!

In the van

The Scillonian parson -apocryphally possibly, in fact, probably - addressed his congregation from the pulpit at the start of a service. "Brethren" he said gravely "It is my sad duty to inform you there has been a shipwreck". Before he could get any further, he found he was speaking to an empty church. Years later on entering the church he stopped and again addressed the assembled congregation, "Brethren, it is my sad duty to inform you there has been a wreck and (stripping off his cassock) this time we all start fair!"

Benjamin Franklin

To the 17th century, now disused, lighthouse on St.Agnes is, indirectly, owed the installation of lighthouses in the United States. The great statesman and inventor Benjamin Franklin was once on passage to England when, in bad weather and shipwreck looming, the St.Agnes coal-burning fire was sighted and his ship prevented from going on the rocks. In his autobiography he wrote of his "deliverance" and how he was impressed with "the utility of lighthouses". He resolved "to encourage the building of more of them in America if I should live to return there".

The first Tall Ships

In 1956 the very first Tall Ships Race took place - to Lisbon - and one of the cadets aboard the *Moyana* was a teenage Scillonian. On her passage home the vessel hit heavy weather, sank and her crew had to abandon ship. They were landed at Fowey. Later they were given a civic reception at Southampton. When the Pathe News screened the incident in the then island's cinema, the Plaza, the audience got to their feet and applauded. John Nicholls is now the island's marine pilot.

Election-free zone

The public meeting in St.Mary's Town Hall held by a major political party in the run-up to the General Election drew a disappointing attendance substantiating the view that Scilly was an "Election- Free" Zone. There were more people on the podium than in the hall. Suddenly a head poked itself around the door wanting to get in out of the rain. "Come in sir, come in" enthused the prospective Member of Parliament, desperate for an audience. The newcomer declared his relevance to island politics by announcing he was a vicar from Harrow. They closed the meeting and all went to the pub.

Honk honk

A none-too-popular mainlander resided for a short spell near a Scillonian blind corner. Vehicles approaching from one direction would honk. Vehicles approaching from the other would honk. Situated in mid-honk he was driven bananas. A mirror on the wall failed to solve the problem. Motorists ignored it, kept honking and redoubled their honking, as a matter of course. He got the distinct impression that everyone was getting in his or her car just to honk at his corner. Before he abandoned Scilly he presented his motoring blueprint for St.Mary's. Everyone should drive one-way around the island in milk floats. He neglected to say whether they should be honkless or not!

Small beer!

The former Wing Commander, resplendent in yachting cap, blazer and squadron tie, cut a colourful figure as he presented awards at the annual Carnival Sports on the St.Mary's Garrison. "First prize", he boomed, "two candelabra". There was a stunned silence broken by a hoarse whisper. "For goodness sake, George, two CANS OF LAGER"!

Cable's length

The coming to hitherto isolated Scilly of the telegraph cable in 1869 was a red-letter day for the islands. The whole of St.Mary's assembled at Deep Point to see its arrival and celebrate a major connection with the big outside world. What they didn't know was that the cable - from Land's End - had proved to be too short! Unseen and further out to sea they had severed it and towed the fag end ashore before a blissfully unaware audience! The re-connection was done later.

The Marcos speedboat

The sleek, e x p e n s i v e, p o w e r f u l speedboat at her moorings in St.Mary's Pool belonged to Prince Charles and won many an admiring glance from both visitors and Islanders even if it was rarely used. Twenty-eight foot long, with a 330 hp engine and capable of doing 45 mph, it was something of an embarrassment, however - not because of its luxuriousness but because of its origins. It had been the gift of discredited Philippines dictator Ferdinand Marcos and his profligate wife Imelda. It was, therefore, not a politically correct speedboat and had to go. It did.

Beach landing

One of the very first planes to ever land in Scilly did so just three years after Lindbergh's pioneering 1927 transatlantic flight in "Spirit of St.Louis". This, too, was a transatlantic crossing. A Bellanca monoplane "Columbia" emergency - landed on the sand of Pentle Beach, Tresco, having experienced fuel problems with a plugged oil line. It had flown from Newfoundland although pilot Captain Errol Boyd and navigator Lieutenant Harry Connor had originally started out in Montreal. The crossing of 2,200 miles took 23.5 hours. Fuel was sent from the mainland and the plane eventually landed at Croydon.

Two of the few

The Penzance-Scilly helicopter service, operated by British International, is the only scheduled commercial helicopter service in the world, while the Isles of Scilly Steamship Company's *RMV Scillonian III* has been described by "Ships Monthly" as "one of the world's last coastal passenger/cargo vessels".

The Welcome Stranger

The biggest gold nugget ever found was done so on February 5, 1869 by a Scillonian, John Deason, formerly of Tresco. He was in Moliagul, Victoria, following a spell prospecting in the Bendigo Goldfields. His pick struck something hard under the roots of a tree. It was a gold nugget which, when unearthed, was so large that it had to be transported by cart. A bank's scales could not cope with the weight. A blacksmith reduced it with hammer and chisel. It is known to posterity as "The Welcome Stranger". Sharing the find with Deason was his colleague, Richard Oates, a Cornishman.

Driving tests

Driving tests are taken on St.Mary's despite the absence of features standard to the mainland - like roundabouts, crossings, one-way systems, lights, indeed traffic! An examiner comes over from the mainland. When the theory section of the test was first introduced there was consternation. Unlike the test proper it could not be done in Scilly. Would-be drivers were faced with a costly mainland trip. They could drive at home, but had to go away to theorise! Eventually it was agreed the theory test could be sat in the islands.

Traffic jam

An island lady driver used to get into a pickle when called upon to reverse, which made it difficult when in a narrow lane leading from her home she would regularly meet the dustcart. They would still be stationary looking at each other to this day if the refuse man, with unfailing courtesy, had not dismounted his vehicle every time and taken over her controls!

Revenge

A well-loved Scillonian guesthouse keeper, the late Ena Reseigh, was taken aback when new arrivals shouted at her and jumped on a chair every time her meek little dog entered the room. Bus driver Vic Trenwith had told them, in jest, that they would have to speak up as she was very deaf and be careful of her fierce dog. She gained her revenge. Incognito in wig and dark glasses she secreted herself aboard Vic's round-island tour bus proclaiming "rubbish" at every one of Vic's anecdotes!

Security scare

A major security scare developed one lazy summer day in the 1960s when the then Prime Minister Harold Wilson was in Scilly on leave, when a holidaymaker - who claimed to be an Irish peer - told a member of an hotel's staff that he had a gun in his baggage and could easily assassinate the PM. A task force flew in from the mainland. The holidaymaker was apprehended, his room searched. He did indeed have a firearm and a licence for it. He really was an Irish peer, albeit of an a somewhat eccentric bent. He was deported. Flap over.

Tallest lighthouse

The tallest lighthouse in the British Isles is the Bishop Rock, six miles to the west of the islands. It has a chequered history. The first structure of cast iron was erected in 1849 and washed away in a storm the following year, before it could be used. The second suffered from chronic vibrations. An outer casing was put on to sheathe it and a further two storeys were added. It now stands some 175 feet above sea level, but in storms spray hits the top and the mercury holding the lens has been spilt. A helicopter-landing pad was put on top in 1976. It is now unmanned and has an automatically controlled beam that can be seen at sea for 25 miles. During its construction workmen lived on the tiny island among the western rocks, Rosevear, where it is said that one night they had an open-air ball!

The talkies

The cinema age came to Scilly when Mr Bert Ashford started showing silent films in the Church Hall via car-battery generation! The "talkies", under the same management, came at the Atlantic Hotel, Hugh Town, St.Mary's in 1934 with the film "Rome Express". Later a purpose-built cinema was built in Garrison Lane - the Plaza, the programme being changed twice a week. Like so many cinemas it fell victim to television in the early 1970s. The building was subsequently demolished, the site first being used as a car park. It is now occupied by council housing. There is now no cinema in Scilly.

Scilly of the South Seas

The Isles of Scilly are not the only island archipelago bearing that name in the world. Cornish mariner Captain Wallis, who sailed with Captain Cook and was one of the 18th century's famous sailors, named an atoll in the Society Islands in the South Pacific the Scilly Islands. Being familiar with Scillonian waters, it is probable that certain physical similarities determined his choice of name, although it has been suggested the name might have honoured a Scillonian seaman who sailed with Wallis. There is also a Scilly Isles traffic island on the Kingston by-pass.

All sewn up!

Tregarthen's, Scilly's oldest hotel, represented the perfect commercial if somewhat monopolistic arrangement for its 19th century owner and founder, the legendary Captain Frank Tregarthen. He was Master, successively, of the packet boats *Ariadne* and *Little Western*. His mainland guests could not check out of his hotel until he decided to sail. It is darkly said they could not book a passage to the islands unless they were going to stay at Tregarthen's and that any sailing for replenishment of island stores hinged on the state of the hotel larder!

Tresco Abbey Garden

The sub-tropical Garden at Tresco, started in 1835 by the architect of modern Scilly, Augustus Smith and thereafter extended and cherished by successive Dorrien-Smiths, is world famous. Exotic trees and plants from all over the world flourish, uniquely, for northern climes. In the early years many species were brought home from abroad by Scillonian mariners.

Distress and famine

Scilly has not always been "The Fortunate Islands". Distress visited them nearly 50 years before the mid-19th century Irish famine, particularly the off-islands whose misery was said to be "extreme". The begging bowl was held out to Penzance for relief. One of the reasons for the penury was the successful suppression of smuggling which had proved an island staple, and the collapse of piloting, kelp-making and harvests. The islanders' plight even found its way into the columns of "The Times". It is said that the sternboard of wrecked Admiral Sir Clowdisley Shovell's *HMS Association* now rests in a magistrates court at St.John's Hall, Penzance in exchange for help in time of need.

Barren and dreary

Scilly was "a dreary, barren place" to John Wesley when he visited St.Mary's for the one and only time in 1743. He sailed there on a boat lent him by the Mayor of St.Ives and such was the length and roughness of the voyage that Wesley and his party had to resort to hymn singing to keep their spirits up. He held some open-air meetings in Hugh Town, idly watched by "sullen" islanders and got out of the place as soon as he could. Scilly did not reciprocate in kind, however, to Wesley's dismissive assessment of it. His message took root. Some 50 years later the Wesleyan Chapel in Hugh Town was built and Methodism in the islands has remained strong ever since.

Nicknames

Each Scillonian island has a name for its inhabitants, rooted in the mists of history and now rarely used save for St.Agnes and St.Martin's. The former's folk are "Turks" after their traditional swarthy, moustachioed appearance while Tresco natives are "Caterpillars" in deference, perhaps, to a smuggling past when lines of men would pass barrels on moonlit nights. Bryher folk are "Thorns", St.Martin's, inexplicably, are "Ginnicks" while St.Mary's - also for reasons unknown - are "Bulldogs".

The lady and the tramps

The Royal retinue accompanying a fleeing Prince Charles during the Civil War in 1646 holed up in Scilly and was glad to get out of the place six weeks later. A Lady Fanshawe, pregnant in the most difficult of circumstances, tells us she came ashore "almost dead" after being sick and "pillaged" by the seamen. While the Prince presumably had reasonable accommodation high up in the Star Castle, the good lady was menially quartered further down among the common folk. It was "so vile that my footman even lay in a better". She complained of the smell of fish, lack of clothing and food, the cold and of nearly being drowned by a spring tide. "Truly we begged our daily bread of God for we thought every meal our last". But Scilly saved her employer's life. He became king 14 years later.

Puffin rent

Scilly's value in the 14th century was estimated in puffin rent. Ranulph Blancminster was granted the islands by King Edward I in return for paying 300 puffins or six shillings and eight pence. Hard cash was usually exchanged rather than the birds which, nevertheless, were prized for their feathers as well as food.

Scilly's oldest building

The only Grade One Listed building in Scilly is Star Castle on St.Mary's. Constructed in 1593 on the orders of Queen Elizabeth it is in the form of an eight-pointed star and was intended as a defence against a possible second Armada - the first having been repulsed five years earlier. Renowned architect Professor Richardson, in his 1924 "Regional Architecture of the West of England", calls it the most perfect example of Elizabethan castle building there is. But no sooner had it been completed than it was obsolete. The threat had passed. It was subsequently variously used as headquarters for the military and the Duchy of Cornwall. It is now an hotel.

In the teeth of temptation

As a child Tony Mumford would shelter from Luftwaffe aerial attack at Longstone, the St.Mary's farm his family and forebears had held for 300 years. Some 40 years later, as a dentist with the British military in West Germany, he one day found himself being given cover as opposed to taking it when tending to the dentures of one of the architects of his childhood discomfort. His surgery was ringed by troops for - Rudolph Hess! He resisted any temptation to get even.

The first steamer

For many years Scilly was served by a motley flotilla of vessels chartered by the Isles of Scilly Steamship Company. In 1926 the first purpose-built steamer was launched for the company on Clydeside. Door-to-door collections in the islands helped raise funds. A certain Methodist lay-preacher was a major force.

It is said he would spend a minute on a formal sermon and the rest on the Gospel According to the Steamship Company! A well-loved islander Vic Trenwith, of "Vic's Tours" fame who as a boy used to play the bugle in the Town Band, would station himself at Peninnis Head with his bugle to assist the skipper to find his bearings in fog.

The tourist trade

While it is impossible to define the moment Scilly hitched itself to tourism as a staple form of income - it theoretically began in the 19th century when the railhead arrived at Penzance. A significant year was 1949 when the Duchy of Cornwall sold the freehold of Hugh Town to the sitting tenants who, in taking pride in their own property as opposed to someone else's, started "taking in visitors". A fledgling tourist trade was born. It is now some 85% of Scilly's livelihood and rising.

Famous Scillonian

Scillonians have moved out into all corners of the world to make good and one who can lay valid claim to have been Scilly's most famous son was ship's carpenter Henry Trevellick. Whether the long hours spent during the 19th century heyday of Scillonian shipbuilding were the prime motivation, is not known, but what is known is that he emigrated to Detroit in the United States, became an advocate of the eight-hour day, was a pioneer in the US labour union movement and a leading architect of Labor Day.

Royal seat

The chairman of the Isles of Scilly Council sits on a royal throne even if he is a commoner. His ornately-carved oak chair was used by Prince Charles - later to be King Charles II, at the 1660 Restoration - when fleeing from the Roundheads to Scilly during the Civil War. The chair was variously used by freemasons and royalty - the Duke of Windsor took it to Fort Belvedere - before it was brought back to Scilly and into the Town Hall Council Chamber. It is known as Prince Charles' Chair.

Election Day in Scilly

General Election polling day is different in Scilly. Even when the voting sheet tells the official-in-charge that the handful of eligible voters have all polled he or she still has to keep the booth open until the prescribed hour! Then the votes are brought down from the various off-islands by boat, kept overnight in the one cell at the police station (with the police bike for company) and then flown out to Penzance to be subsumed in the greater St.Ives Division ballot. In organising the transfer of the ballot papers from the off-islands to St.Mary's the Returning Officer must keep his weather eye on the tide.

Ship's cook twice in the stew!

In 1927 an Italian steamer *S.S.Isabo*, out of the musically sounding port of Lussinpicolo, was wrecked on Scilly Rock. One of the rescued was the ship's cook. Coxswain of the lifeboat who saved him was the late Matt Lethbridge. Twenty-eight years later on a rock not far from Scilly Rock called the Golden Ball - a Panamanian steamer the Mando was wrecked. Among the rescued was - the very same ship's cook! Leading the rescuers was - the very same Matt Lethbridge! To have been shipwrecked twice within hailing distance of the same spot and to be saved twice by the same man must constitute something of a record.

Managed retreat - or "let it drown"

Erosion is inexorably reducing low-lying Scilly's acreage and is only contained when coastal defence works - shored up by money from the Ministry of Agriculture, Fisheries and Food (MAAF) - are periodically and expensively put in place. Financial justification for these works is linked to an equation showing what is to be saved exceeds the cost of the saving. Scilly's glory - miles of wild, open cliffscape - is therefore doomed. It is seen as valueless. The authorities are expected to pursue a policy of "managed retreat", a nice little euphemism for "let it drown".

How flying started

The first air services to Scilly were provided in 1937 by Channel Air Ferries of the Olley Air Services company and Great Western and Southern Airlines. The aircraft was a de Havilland Dragon and flew from Kelynack, St.Just in Cornwall. Fixed-wing flying continued on the route, under British European Airways who took over in 1947 until the present helicopter link was established in 1964 at Penzance. St.Just is now used by the Isles of Scilly Skybus Company's Britten-Norman Islander aircraft.

Early Luftwaffe target

Tiny Scilly was under attack by the Luftwaffe in the Second World War well before most parts of mainland Britain. Targets were the radio stations at both Peninnis and Newford, both on St.Mary's. Three people died in the islands during the conflict due to enemy raids. Two women were killed in the house "Bonavista", St.Mary's when it took a direct bomb hit. A young girl in the coastguard tower at Telegraph Hill lost her life when machined-gunned by a German plane.

Scilly's "White House"

During the premiership of Scilly's most celebrated ratepayer, Labour leader Harold, later to be Lord, Wilson the customs building on the St.Mary's Strand was converted to accommodate sophisticated communications equipment. The "Scillonian No 10" or the "Western White House" was used in such crises as Vietnam, the Rhodesian secession, the Torrey Canyon oil tanker affair and many others.

Lyonesse Remembrance League

Scilly kept the home fires burning for all islanders absent serving in the Second World War. An organisation called "The Lyonesse Remembrance League" sent regular letters to each sailor, soldier, airman and men and women serving in other capacities wherever they were, home or abroad, containing, amongst other things sweets, cigarettes and the current issue of the islands' publication "The Scillonian".

A prophet hath no honour

Labour PM Harold Wilson was undoubtedly a great ally for Scilly during his premiership. It seemed delegations from the Islands' council invariably cut through layers of bureaucratic "red tape" to see the people that mattered at Westminster and it was largely through his influence that Tonga bought the Steamship Company's vessel *The Queen of the Isles*. Yet the council not once, but four times, threw out planning applications for modest renovations to his St.Mary's bungalow "Lowenva".

NAAFI

During the war the servicemen's NAAFI was situated on St.Mary's quay in what is now the Harbourside Hotel. But they had to shift to Holgate's Hotel on the Strand. Too many were walking out of the NAAFI door, over the side of the quay and straight into the drink!

In the family

The most famous lifeboat family in the long history of the St.Mary's RNLI branch is the Lethbridge's. They have provided more than one highly decorated coxswain and at one stage there were no fewer than five family members in the crew at the same time with a sixth on the slip. Now there are none.

A medical man

A quiet, self-effacing and most pleasant medical man used to regularly come to Scilly in the earlier years of this century, stay at Tregarthen's Hotel on St.Mary's and go boating. The locals liked him. History doesn't. He was Dr Crippen.

Bunkered

The president of the Isles of Scilly Golf Club was fairly bursting with the importance of the occasion. Among the revellers at the club's New Year's Eve bash in the old Wesleyan Chapel was none other than the Prime Minister Harold Wilson. The president's build-up to the climactic moment of welcome was laborious, pompous and long-winded which only served to accentuate the gaffe: "It gives me great pleasure to welcome the Rt Honourable Harold ...Macmillan."

Population breakdown

At the height of the holiday season Scilly's population is more than doubled, but the resident total of 2048 - based on figures from the last census - is broken down as follows: St.Mary's, 1607; Tresco, 167; St.Martin's, 113; St.Agnes, 83; Bryher, 78. A former trend, which saw the off-islands losing their population, has been reversed.

This sporting life

Adaptability is a necessary attribute if you are to enjoy your sport in Scilly. Hence you play tennis on some tarmacadam in a disused quarry; soccer against the same team each week, every week; squash in a court whose roof until

recently was too low and whose floor was the dance floor from a demolished hotel; you shoot in a prefab hut in an old 19th century fort; you play cricket (on Tresco) on a helicopter landing ground; run round and round in circles if you're training for the marathon; strap gig paddles to the soccer posts if you play rugby; risk knocking yourself out on a too low room roof when you trampoline. But all these things are surely to be expected in a blessed world where you once booked your tennis at the dairy, held your Squash Club AGM in the doctor's waiting room and if you want your shoes mended you went to the hairdressers!

Party non-political

A political party wanted to increase their strength in Scilly, so to seduce islanders into signing up, they laid on food and drink in the Town Hall and invited them to the bash. The MP was present with other party grandees. The Scillonians duly turned up in force, gave a pretty good impression of a flock of starving gannets - and consumed the grub and the booze in quick time. But not the message: the party retreated, licking its wounds. Its strength on Scilly remained at two.

Inter - island walk

So much of Scilly has drowned over the centuries - and, indeed, still is drowning - that it is possible to walk between all the islands when tides are suitable barring St.Agnes in the west, which lies in deeper water. On a low spring one can walk from Samson to Bryher to Tresco to St.Martin's and then on to Bar, St.Mary's although the last stretch, with the tide "making", is perhaps best tackled by a sixfooter-plus.

They lived on Samson

Twin-hilled Samson, now an archetypal desert isle, was once inhabited by two families: the Webbers and the Woodcocks, living was at subsistence level. Various tales tell of its depopulation in the 19th century. One says the new Lord Proprietor Augustus Smith, in his ruthless, albeit successful, drive to make the Scillonian economy viable, drove them out. Another maintains that all able-bodied Samson men went down in a shipwreck. It is said the two families had originally upped from St.Mary's and crossed the Roadstead after a long running feud with the Banfield and Mumford families. Samson is the location of the Victorian melodrama "Armorel of Lyonesse" regarded by many as still Scilly's definitive novel. The ruins of "Armorel's Cottage" are still there. Samson was once used as the backdrop for a film "Treasure Island".

Switch off

When the St.Mary's Electric Light Company first started operating in Warsall's Quarry on St.Mary's in the 1930s - the site of today's power station - it was decided to switch off at midnight as an economy measure. To warn householders of the impending curfew the lights were dimmed just before they totally went. That's service for you!

The Mal de Mers

In the 1930s Scilly's isolation prevented sporting contact with the outside world, so when a team came from Plymouth and played hockey it was quite an event. That team grew into a club calling itself the Mal de Mers after its initial

sickly voyage on the *RMS Scillonian* - which they thereafter called the "Hell Ship" - and has been coming back annually ever since. In a five-day blitz it plays the islanders at everything - from cricket to soccer, darts to snooker, gig rowing to clay- pigeon shooting. One of its early touring members was a gentleman called William Joyce. He didn't come again. He was Lord Haw Haw.

Christian conversion

It is said Christianity was brought to Scandinavia as a direct result of events in Scilly. Norway's king Olav Treggvyssen, on a pillaging cruise, was converted by St.Elide on the Scillonian isle of St.Helen's which to this day has the remains of a medieval priory. The story comes from Snorri Sturlason in "The Heimskringla".

The "Sol"

The staple - and most famous - flower grown in Scilly is the *Tazetta aurea*, better known as the Soleil d'Or, or, simply, the "Sol". It is said to have been brought to the islands by French sailors.

Shipbuilding

The halcyon years for Scilly, in general economic terms, were the mid-1800s when a thriving local shipbuilding industry was conducted on St.Mary's. There were two yards above the Town Beach on the Strand and two at Porthcressa. Hugh Town was alive with sailmakers, shipwright apprentices, riggers, carpenters and caulkers. Local ships, with Scillonian Masters and Scillonian crews, traded the world's sea routes - to the Baltic, the Black Sea, the Azores and the Med; to Australia and New Zealand; to North and South Americas bringing home a range of cargo from timber to fruit; from wool to meat. The biggest ship to be built in Scilly was the *John Banfield* at 528 tons. The last Porthcressa ship was the *David Auterson* (1870); the last Town Beach ship was the *Gleaner* (1878). The advent of steam ended an era, which was the high tide of Scillonian prosperity until the coming of the flower industry and more recently, the tourist trade.

Famine years

If there is any antipathy between the off-islands and St.Mary's - as opposed to a natural and healthy rivalry - then it most probably has its roots in the depression years of the early 19th century. The off-islanders endured severe hardship. Crops failed, pilotage and kelp-making declined, smuggling - a traditional pursuit - was squeezed. They faced, and endured, penury living off limpets on the very edge of famine. More prosperous, more commercial St.Mary's is not on record as assisting its brethren overmuch and it was only overtures to Penzance, letters in "The Times" and mainland philanthropy which averted total disaster.

Pilotage

Today's pilot gigs, raced by islanders, recall the days when they were used for what their name suggests - placing pilots aboard home-bound ships. Great rivalry existed between the respective crews and respective islands to get the prize - and the remuneration. All islands had their pilot gigs and their crews who would race to launch at the sight of a "Jack": a signal that a ship needed their services. Most westerly St.Agnes was ideally positioned and was always known as the "Pilot's Island". Situated at the crossroads of the English Channel, the Irish Sea and the Atlantic, Scilly was ideally placed for pilotage. The oldest gig being used today is the 1830-built *Bonnet*. The *Slippen* dates from 1869, the *Czar* from 1879. The *Shah* came to Scilly in 1873.

Lily rash

A particularly nasty - and most painful - allergy associated down the years with those employed in the Scillonian flower fields is what is known as "Lily Rash". The sap causes some hands, although by no means all, to swell and crack. This can in some cases can be totally disabling. It is an occupational hazard of the trade.

Refuse disposal

Refuse disposal is inevitably a headache in islands dedicated to tourism. Gone are the days when dumping in the sea is allowed. A Council incinerator on St.Mary's is used. Off-island rubbish is shipped down to St.Mary's to be burnt, although this is a fairly recent measure. Previously each island - they are all owned by Prince Charles' Duchy of Cornwall - had its own dump, which increasingly contradicted the Area of Outstanding Natural Beauty and Heritage Coast labels slapped on them. The rub came when a national tabloid carried a picture of the St.Martin's Wine Cove tip with the headline "How Green is Your Valley, Charles?"

The town hall swingometer

In the pre-desalination plant days the Council's then Chief Technical Officer Brian Lowen would keep a close eye on water levels by using a gadget resembling the General Election "swingometer" beloved of TV. He would erect the graph outside the Town Hall indicating the falling levels, danger zones, safety areas, but whenever TV came across to film it the heavens opened. It was known as Brian's "Rain Dance". The desalination plant has prevented the annual lurch into shortage, but Scillonians are warned that it does not allow for excess.

The airport plaque

The plaque on the wall of the terminal building of St.Mary's Airport grandly announced with the seriousness due to the occasion, that the new amenities had been officially opened by HRH The Duchess of Kent. The trouble is they hadn't or at least not when it claimed she had. She was 30 miles away stuck on the mainland, stranded by Scillonian travel's archenemy fog! Belated validity came to the plaque a few months later when the Duchess actually made it!

Upright to the end

In the years between the wars a clever, albeit eccentric borough engineer came to Scilly and took the lease of Gugh which, sporadically, when tide dictates, assumes the status of a full island when the sandbar linking it with St.Agnes is covered. Islanders were not surprised, perhaps, when his will decreed he should be interred on his beloved Gugh, although the time - dawn - intrigued. It was the mode of burial that puzzled - standing up! The theory was advanced that he believed the perpendicular would give him a head start when the Call came from Him. Not to be outdone St.Mary's also claims its upright burial. In Old Town churchyard there is a grave of ship's surgeon Abraham Leggatt who also favoured the perpendicular.

A royal connection?

Holgate's Hotel which was situated on the St.Mary's Strand and was pulled down in the 1970s, was owned by an autocratic Scillonian Group Captain "Teddy" Burling, a pioneer aviator and skilled yachtsman. He mysteriously came to Scilly as a baby at the turn of the last century with his mother (later to marry a Scillonian) and grew up to have social connections far beyond the scope of his contemporary islanders. He bore an extraordinary and uncanny likeness to the man who later became King Edward VIII.

Off line

The local golfer on the St.Mary's links was good but desperately slow and deliberate. One day at a certain hole he uncharacteristically pushed his ball into the gorse out of bounds. When asked what had happened he confessed he was mystified as he had done what he had always done - lined up on the mast of the steamer *Scillonian*. The trouble was he had taken so long to play the shot that the ship had put to sea.

The Troytown Maze

Europe comes to an end on the western shore of St. Agnes with just the vastness of the Atlantic Ocean separating it from the Americas. Here, on this lonely littoral is a pattern of stones worked into the turf above the shoreline forming a maze or a labyrinth. It is said similar patterns exist elsewhere in the world - and in antiquity – but the general consensus suggests it was constructed in the early 1700s by a bored lighthouse keeper.

Erin's loss, Scillonia's gain

Ireland's loss was Scilly's gain. Augustus Smith, the benevolent autocrat widely recognised as the architect of the today's relative well-being in the islands, came perilously close to not taking up the lease of Scilly in the 1830s. He was seriously flirting with a similar challenge in Ireland and only came to an agreement with the Duchy of Cornwall at the very last minute. Any indecision ceased forthwith as he took steps to put an end to a miserable subsistence-style living on the off-islands and put the islands on the road to order and prosperity.

425 days in an open boat

One of the greatest feats of endurance in adversity must fall to a Scillonian, Eric Goddard, a St.Martin's man. In 1923 he was an Officer Apprentice on the Hain line freighter *Trevessa* carrying a cargo of zinc from Freemantle to Durban. She sank in the Indian Ocean. With 53 other seamen he took to one of two open boats with no clothing, little water or food in one of the greatest ocean vastnesses in the world. He drifted for 25 days and not far short of 2000 miles before landfall. The men's feet and hands swelled, they broke out in boils, and one man went delirious through drinking salt water and died. Altogether eleven died. Back home they thought he had perished. But Eric Goddard survived and never went to sea again.

Sally the seal

The first time Scilly really hit the national headlines in the modern era was when a grey Atlantic seal surfaced into a rubber car tyre and couldn't get it off. Soon papers, TV and radio were bringing regular bulletins of Sally the Seal and her fight for life. Being unable to submerge she could not feed. Soon a mate was cooked up - Sammy the Seal - and on it went. The story had a happy ending. Sally managed to shed the rubber and dived into history.

Democracy

Democracy came late to Scilly - as recently as the 50s. Since the birth of the Isles of Scilly Council in 1891 leadership automatically fell to the Dorrien-Smith family of Tresco Abbey, by an assumed right. Georgie Woodcock, a former engineer on the steamer Scillonian, broke the mould when he became the first elected leader in the authority's history. The wheel turned full circle two decades later however. The late Tom Dorrien-Smith, became chairman by vote.

Shipwreck

Israel Pender was trudging along King Edward's Lane, St.Mary's one early morning minding his own business on his way to milk his cows, when he bumped into a group of men walking along the road in the opposite direction. They were wet and bedraggled. They were survivors from the *Minnehaha*, which had just foundered on the rocks of Peninnis. Something similar occurred many years later with the loss of the *Lady Charlotte* at Porth Hellick. The first anyone knew of it was when survivors knocked on the door of "Normandy House".

Housing Catch 22

Beautiful Scilly is a desirable place to live, but it is small, therefore demand far outstrips supply: a quart wants to get into a pint pot. House prices are artificially high. Local incomes are commensurately low and so most sales go to the mainland. Almost 50% of St.Mary's houses are "second homes", whose owners get a 50% Council Tax discount! Locals inevitably feel the housing squeeze; they have to resort to the over-burdened Council list, which can never fully cope, because if it did - and the Council hasn't the money to build and many of its houses have been lost through Right to Buy anyway - resultant development would adversely affect the island's environment and its appeal, which caused this Catch 22 situation in the very first place.

Great War hero

It is on record that the late Claudevalle (Claudee) Phillips was Scilly's first injured Great War serviceman. When this soldier from the trenches arrived by ship at St.Mary's Quay half the island were there to welcome home their hero. He was carried shoulder high through the town preceded by the Town Band.

Time and tide

The collection-time information at the post box in the St.Mary's "country" was as precise as nature would allow: "According to the tide".

Scillonian millionaire

A Scillonian boy, educated locally on St.Mary's, was after the war, thought to be unexceptional and, indeed, had to "cram" with extra tuition to get through the most standard of examinations. Three decades later, in the most competitive country in the world, Richard Pender was a millionaire! He had established a niche in the US electronics market to such an effect that his initial employer, a global and household player, had to buy him out. Not bad for a lad who hadn't seen a train until he was 16.

First Scilly - mainland swim

The 28-mile stretch of tidal Lyonesse water dividing Scilly and Cornwall -

longer and more treacherous than the English Channel - had never been swum, until August 1998. A City exchange dealer Alison Streeter achieved the feat from Deep Point, St.Mary's to Sennen Cove, Cornwall in a time of 15 hours, 11 minutes, 14 seconds. The following year she tried the east-west route, but failed. After 14 hours in the water, battling strong tides, she gave up. At one stage she was only a tantalizing half mile off the Eastern Isles. A few years earlier another Alison - Alison Roberts, a Welsh swimming pool attendant, had come desperately close to completing this route. She had to be pulled out of the water near the eastern islands and rushed to St.Mary's hospital by speedboat suffering from the seemingly contradictory combination of hypothermia and sunburn.

All on board were asleep!

For the last 35 miles of her doomed voyage, which ended on the rocks of Scilly in March 1997 the container ship *Cita* was crewed by eight men, all of whom were - asleep! A Marine Accidents Investigations Branch (MAIB) Report of the Inquiry into the disaster says the Polish mate dozed off in the Watchman's Chair on the bridge and failed to make the necessary course adjustment, which would have taken the ship safely up the Irish Sea. Meanwhile the Master and entire crew was also asleep. She kept coming and coming at 13 knots until halted by Newfoundland Point, Porth Hellick. Then they woke up!

You'll learn - or else!

Scilly can lay claim to have been the first place in the whole of the British Isles to introduce compulsory education way in advance of the Forster Act of 1870. One of the first things "Lord Proprietor" Augustus Smith did on taking the lease of the islands from the Duchy of Cornwall in the mid-1830s was to insist that island children attended school. To ensure this he charged one old penny for attendance, but two pence for truancy. Few parents could afford their children's absence.

Pub lunch

Not too long ago on Tresco around 12 noon you might have seen an orderly crocodile of children setting off from the local primary school at Old Grimsby on their way to lunch - at the local pub! There were no cooking facilities at the

school at the time so the New Inn had to make do as a somewhat unorthodox school canteen.

The Samson Picnic

Most schools have an annual outing and those in Scilly are no different. However the venue for that outing is unique: every child's dream: a Crusoe island. Each year for the past 50 years the islands' primary school children of St.Mary's, St.Agnes, Tresco and St.Martin's have sailed away across the water for a fairytale summer's day out - to Samson - the archetypal desert isle of twin hills where they have rambled among the bracken, explored the ruined cottages, played games on the beach and generally let off steam.

The telephone operator

In the days when all telephone calls had to go through the local exchange on St.Mary's (Scillonia), the operator was known to everybody, knew everybody in return and dispensed an unrivalled service. "He's playing darts at the Club" he would advise,"Try again in an hour or so", or "You won't get her at home, you know it's her WI night. She won't be back until 9.30", or " I think I saw Dad going to a Council meeting". Highly irregular, but highly appreciated.

For those in peril

Observers afloat off Tresco a few years ago were intrigued by the sight of a motor boat hard aground stuck on a low-tide sand bar. Her crew, trousers rolled up, were knee-deep in the water, desperately striving to tow her off, while one person - a big man under a capacious Panama hat - orchestrated things from inboard barking a string of instructions to the toilers. Holidaying Rev Ian Paisley was finding out at first hand what it was like to be in peril on the sea.